Contents

KU-754-294

Some words are shown in bold, **like this**. You can find out what they mean by looking in the glossary.

 Find out more about scooters and skateboards at www.heinemannexplore.co.uk

Scooters and skateboards

This boy is riding a scooter.

handlebar

Scooters and skateboards are toys with wheels. You can use them to move without walking. Scooters have handlebars to help you **balance**.

How do they work?

Scooters and Skateboards

Wendy Sadler

www.heinemann.co.uk/library

Visit our website to find out more information about **Heinemann Library** books.

To order:

 Phone 44 (0) 1865 888066

 Send a fax to 44 (0) 1865 314091

 Visit the Heinemann Bookshop at www.heinemann.co.uk/library to browse our catalogue and order online.

First published in Great Britain by Heinemann Library, Halley Court, Jordan Hill, Oxford OX2 8EJ, part of Harcourt Education.
Heinemann is a registered trademark of Harcourt Education Ltd.

Editorial: Andrew Farrow and Dan Nunn
Design: Ron Kamen and Dave Oakley/
  Arnos Design
Picture Research: Hannah Taylor
Production: Duncan Gilbert
Originated by Ambassador Litho Ltd
Printed and bound in China by
South China Printing Company.

The paper used to print this book comes from sustainable resources.

0 431 04969 6
09 08 07 06 05
10 9 8 7 6 5 4 3 2 1

British Library Cataloguing in Publication Data

Sadler, Wendy
  Scooters and skateboards. – (How do they work?)
  1. Scooters – Design and construction – Juvenile literature
  2. Skateboards – Design and construction – Juvenile literature
  I. Title
  685.3'62

A full catalogue record for this book is available from the British Library.

Acknowledgements
The publishers would like to thank the following for permission to reproduce photographs: Actionplus (Tim Leighton-Boyce) p. **28**; Buzz Pictures (Mike John) p. **29**; Corbis pp. **10** (Jim Cummins), **21** (Larry Kasperrek/NewSport), **22** (Aaron Chang), **23** (Duomo), **27** (Duomo); Creatas p. **4**; Harcourt Education Ltd (Tudor Photography) pp. **5**, **6**, **7**, **8**, **9**, **12**, **13**, **14**, **15**, **16**, **17**, **18**, **19**, **20**, **24**, **25**; Imagestate (Michael Paras) p. **11**; Stockfile p. **26**.

Cover photograph reproduced with permission of Harcourt Education Ltd (Tudor Photography).

Every effort has been made to contact copyright holders of any material reproduced in this book. Any omissions will be rectified in subsequent printings if notice is given to the publishers.

Skateboards do not have handlebars. They are harder to ride. Some people can do jumps on a skateboard.

What is a scooter?

All scooters have a footplate for you to stand on. Most scooters have three wheels, but some have two or four. Scooters are usually made of metal or plastic.

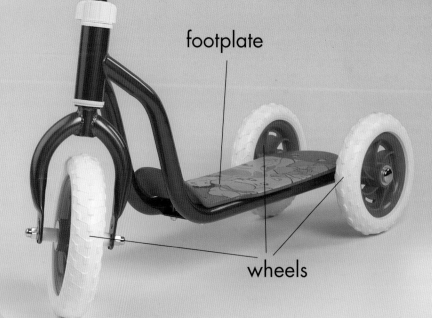

footplate

wheels

handlebar

front wheel

There is a handlebar at the front of a scooter. The handlebar is joined to the front wheel. You turn the handlebar so you can go around corners.

Scooter wheels

A scooter runs on wheels. A scooter without wheels would scrape or rub against the ground. This rubbing is called **friction**. Friction would stop the scooter from moving.

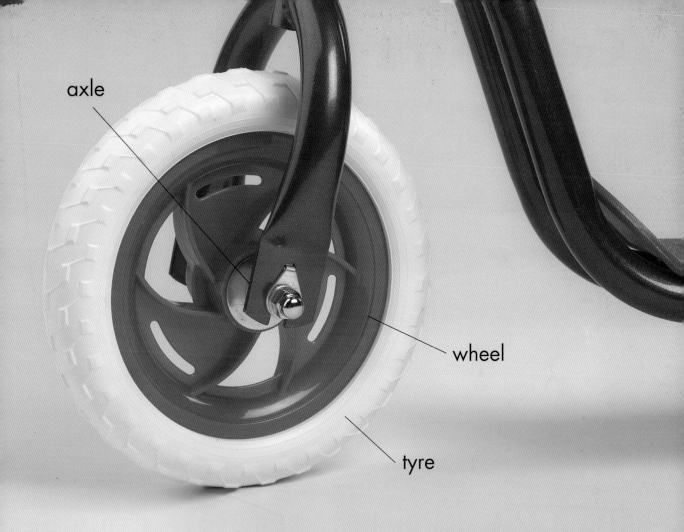

axle

wheel

tyre

The wheels are joined to an **axle**. The axle is in the middle of the wheel. The wheel turns around the axle. If the wheels were stuck to the scooter they would not move around.

Getting moving

To get moving you need to push with your foot. Your foot pushes backwards against the ground. The scooter moves forwards.

you push backwards

the scooter moves forwards

To go faster you have to push harder with your foot. To keep moving you have to keep pushing your foot against the ground.

push

Slowing down

friction stops the scooter from moving

If you stop pushing, the scooter slows down. The wheels rub on the ground and against the **axles**. This rubbing is called **friction**. Friction is a **force** that stops things from moving.

You can use your foot to slow down or stop. If you let your foot rub against the ground there is more friction. With more friction you will stop more quickly.

What is a skateboard?

axle

wheels

A skateboard has four wheels. The wheels are joined to the skateboard by **axles**. A skateboard does not have a handlebar. You have to **balance** on the skateboard.

rough surface

The top of a skateboard is rough to touch. This helps the bottom of your shoes to **grip** the skateboard. If the skateboard was smooth you would slip off!

Making a skateboard move

you push backwards

To ride a skateboard you need good **balance**. You put one foot on the skateboard and use the other foot to push against the ground. When your foot pushes backwards, the skateboard moves forwards.

If you want to go up a hill, you need to push hard. If you are going down a hill, the skateboard rolls down easily. This is because a force called **gravity** pulls it down.

Going round corners

pushing down on one side makes the skateboard turn

A skateboard does not have a handlebar to turn the wheels. To go round a corner you **lean** in the direction you want to go. You push down on one side of the skateboard to make it turn.

You use your **weight** to make a skateboard change direction. This means you need to have good **balance**. If not, you will fall off!

Jumping

Some people can make a skateboard jump. They push down on the back of the board. The front of the board jumps up in the air.

Some skateboarders use **ramps** to help them jump up in the air. You must be very careful on a skateboard. Jumping on skateboards can be **dangerous**.

Ramps and skateboard parks

Skateboard parks have lots of different **ramps** in them. The ramps have different shapes. People practise tricks and jumps on them.

This ramp is called a half-pipe. It has a
steep slope on both sides. Skateboarders
go very fast down one side and jump up
at the top of the other side.

Crash helmets and padding

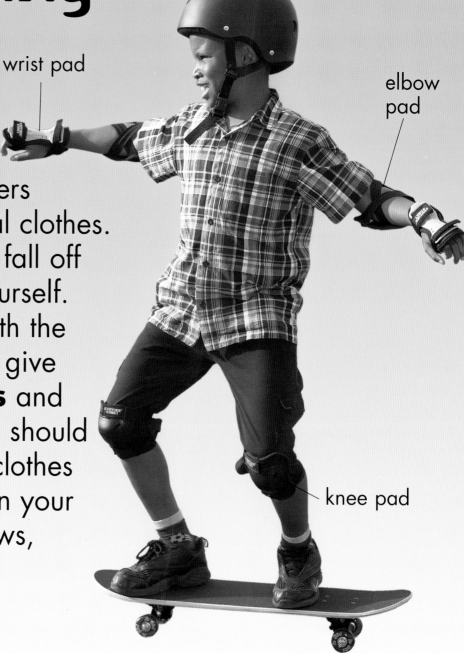

wrist pad

elbow pad

knee pad

Skateboarders need special clothes. It is easy to fall off and hurt yourself. **Friction** with the ground can give you **grazes** and **burns**. You should wear thick clothes and pads on your knees, elbows, and wrists.

helmet

You also need to keep your head safe. A helmet is thick and hard. If you fall on your head, the helmet will stop you from getting badly hurt.

Big wheels

big wheels

Some skateboards and scooters look different. This scooter has big wheels so that you can ride it on rough ground.

This skateboard has big wheels with **rubber tyres**. The wheels are on the side of the skateboard, not under it. This helps riders keep their **balance** on bumpy ground.

tyres

big wheels

27

Fun tricks

Skateboarding can be fun to watch. Look at the tricks this skateboarder is doing!

Find out more about
scooters and skateboards at
www.heinemannexplore.co.uk

29

Glossary

axle rod that holds a wheel, but still lets the wheel turn around

balance ability to stand up without falling over

burn skin injury caused by something that is hot. Friction can produce heat and cause burns.

dangerous not safe, so you could get hurt

force push or pull that makes something move or stops it from moving. Gravity and friction are forces.

friction force of one thing rubbing against another thing

gravity force that pulls everything down towards the ground

graze injury caused by your skin rubbing against something hard

grip hold without slipping

lean move your body to the side

ramp slope that provides a smooth path from a low place to a higher place

rubber tyres tubes filled with air that fit around wheels. They cushion you from bumps in the road.

steep slope slope that needs a lot of work to climb up. Some hills are steep slopes.

weight how heavy something is

Find out more

More books to read

I Can Skateboard, Edana Eckart (Children's Press, 2003)

My World of Science: Forces and Motion, Angela Royston (Heinemann Library, 2001)

The Ultimate Scooter Guide, Ben Sharpe (Scholastic, 2001)

Very Useful Machines: Wheels, Chris Oxlade (Heinemann Library, 2004)

Websites to visit

http://www.exploratorium.edu/skateboarding/
Visit this website to read about the science of skateboarding.

http://www.brainpop.com/
At this website you can watch a film about wheels and then take part in a quiz.

Disclaimer

All the Internet addresses (URLs) given in this book were valid at the time of going to press. However, due to the dynamic nature of the Internet, some addresses may have changed, or sites may have changed or ceased to exist since publication. While the author and Publishers regret any inconvenience this may cause readers, no responsibility for any such changes can be accepted by either the author or the Publishers.

Index

Titles in the *How Do They Work?* series include:

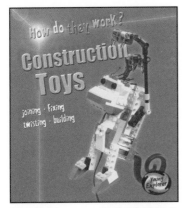

Hardback   0 431 04964 5

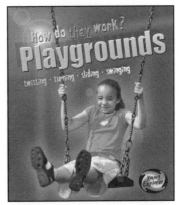

Hardback   0 431 04965 3

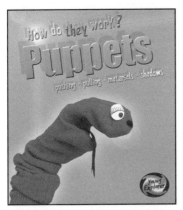

Hardback   0 431 04966 1

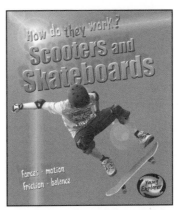

Hardback   0 431 04969 6

Hardback   0 431 04967 X

Hardback   0 431 04968 8

Find out about the other titles in this series on our website www.heinemann.co.uk/library